MARLENE HALPIN, O.P.

THE BALL OF RED
string

A GUIDED MEDITATION FOR CHILDREN

Illustrated by **CARRIE SCHULER**

LOYOLA PRESS.
A JESUIT MINISTRY
Chicago

LOYOLA PRESS.
A JESUIT MINISTRY

www.loyolapress.com

Illustrations by Carrie Schuler
Design by Loyola Press

ISBN: 978-0-8294-5625-7
Library of Congress Control Number: 2009517808

Printed in China
23 24 25 26 27 28 29 30 31 32 DC 10 9 8 7 6 5 4 3 2 1

FOREWORD

When a child loves someone who lives at a distance, the child often begs and begs, "When can we go visit?" As the time to visit approaches, the anticipation heightens. The child gets excited and delighted at what will soon happen. What a fortunate child!

And so it is with every child of God, because every child can be delighted anticipating a visit with Jesus. By using *The Ball of Red String* during prayer time, you can bring to children both the delight of anticipating a visit with Jesus and the grace of some quiet moments alone with him.

This engaging guided meditation is suitable for use at home or in religious education settings, by parents, teachers, or catechists. It offers a proven method of leading children, by awakening their imagination, to a quiet time of meeting Jesus in prayer.

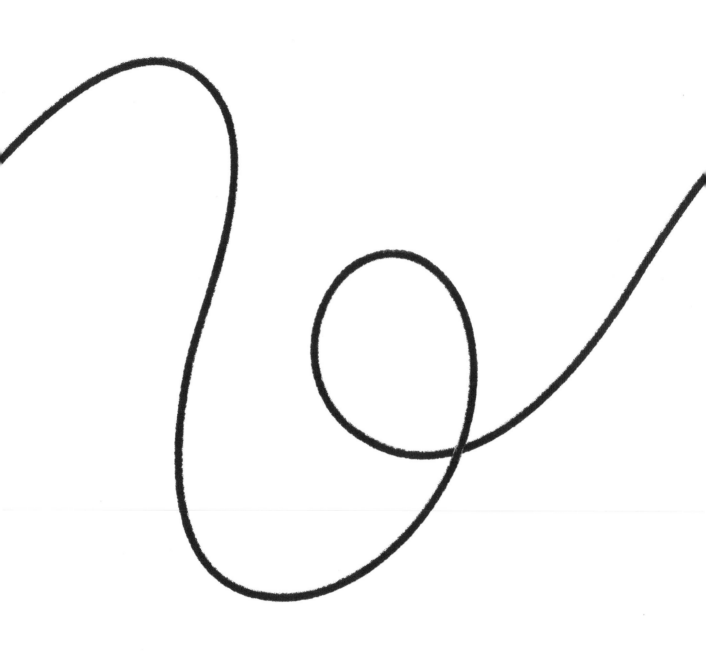

TO BEGIN,

May

TEACHERS

CATECHISTS

CHILDCARE WORKERS

PARENTS

GRANDPARENTS

OTHER FAMILY MEMBERS

BABYSITTERS

enjoy this small book in the companionship of children of all ages.

The Ball of Red String: A Guided Meditation for Children offers a fun and easy way to relax and prepare for prayer. Tips for how to lead this meditation are provided on pages 28–32.

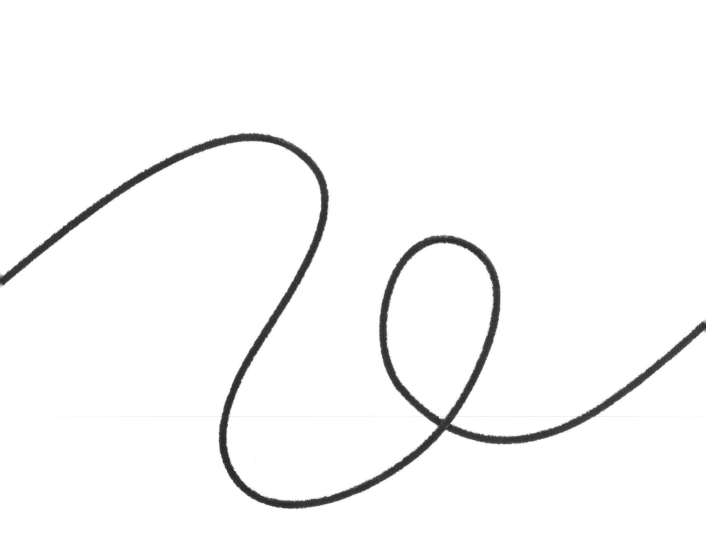

A ball of Red String.

Not many people know why a ball of Red String is so important. You can find out, if you want.

All you have to do is listen and use your imagination.

Imagine yourself walking in a field next to a forest. It is a lovely day. Because anything is possible in your imagination, make it your favorite season of the year. Make it your favorite weather.

You're walking along, all by yourself. It's fun.

As you're walking along enjoying yourself, you get an idea. Somewhere in that forest is a small house. The house has your name on it. It is your Heart Home. You are so sure it is there that you start looking for a pathway to it. You look and look but don't find one.

CATCH!

What you do find is a very large rock.
Perched on the very large rock is an Old
Woman. She is smiling as she looks at you and
says in a very old voice, "You can't find the pathway
to your house, can you?"

"No," you answer.

"Here! Catch!" she says as she tosses you a big ball
of Red String.

When you catch it, she tells you, "Hold the ball of Red String in front of your heart."

You do that, and she tells you to say,

RED STRING, RED STRING,

I WILL FOLLOW YOU, MY RED STRING.

RED STRING, RED STRING,

LET'S GO TO MY HEART HOME!

Then she tells you to toss it out in front of you and follow it.

The Old Woman on the rock sits back, smiling, and watches you.

You take the Red String, hold it in front of your heart, and say,

RED STRING, RED STRING,

I WILL FOLLOW YOU, MY RED STRING.

RED STRING, RED STRING,

LET'S GO TO MY HEART HOME!

And you toss it out in front of you.

The string begins to unravel, rolling along the forest floor. You follow it.

At first, the Red String goes straight ahead under the trees. So do you. It's rolling along slowly enough that you can look up at the trees. You hear birds singing. Can you find one on a tree branch?

You see some very large bushes ahead of you. The Red String goes around them. So do you. Under them there are some bunny rabbits. Do you see them as you walk along?

Now the Red String goes through a clearing in the forest. You walk a little faster. Maybe you catch a glimpse of some deer in the distance.

Oh, what will the Red String do?

Ahead is a big hill of rocks. You wonder if there is any way you can get past it. The Red String goes a little to the right, then finds a hidden pathway. Follow the Red String through the rocks.

You are safe.

You come out into the forest again and keep going. Maybe you are wondering if you will ever get there.

Now there is a river right in front of you. Even if you know how to swim, the river looks awfully wide. Watch your Red String. Watch it very closely.

In some miraculous way, the Red String leads you across the river safely. You even stay dry! How does the Red String transport you across the river? (You don't have to tell anyone what your Red String did, but if you want to later, you can.)

Now your ball of Red String is getting very small. It leads you under some more trees until the ball is completely unwound. Only the curly end of the string is left, sticking up from the ground. Look at it. Then look up.

There it is! Right ahead of you is a clearing, and in the clearing is your house! You are sure of it!

Run over to the house and explore it. Look at it up close. It is such a friendly house.

Come around to the other side. Standing there, waiting for you, is Jesus. You have never seen him before, but you are sure it is Jesus. He smiles, says your name, and tells you he is glad that you came.

Run to Jesus and say hello to him.

Jesus asks you what you want to do. Do you want to explore the inside of the house? Or sit on the porch? Or go for a walk? You and Jesus decide what you want to do.

You do it together.

Jesus is not in a hurry. He has a lot of time and wants to pay attention to you. He wants to listen to you. Jesus asks what you want to talk about.

Take your time. Tell him. Tell him what's happening at home or in school.

Tell Jesus what you think about it and how it makes you feel. With Jesus, you don't have to use words. If you think a lot but can't find the right words to say, invite Jesus to know your mind. He does, of course. You can know things together.

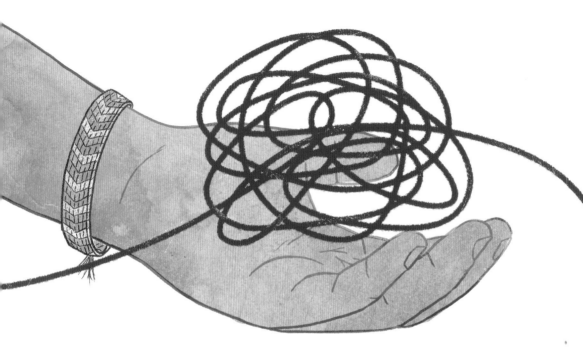

Sometimes the way you feel seems all mixed up. Sometimes it's so good; other times it hurts so much or is so scary that you can't talk about it.

Invite Jesus into your heart so that he can know how your heart feels about things. Jesus can do that. He is so glad to be with you!

Maybe you ask for his advice or help. Remember to be polite and give Jesus time to speak, too.

Be happy just knowing that Jesus understands how it is for you. Take all the time you want to talk with Jesus.

When you are finished, ask Jesus if there is anything he wants you to think about.

Listen with your heart. You probably won't hear any words, but you might know what Jesus means. He's good at giving ideas.

Jesus probably tells you how much God loves you, always. No matter what. Maybe you just sit for a while with Jesus, being happy that you are together.

Then Jesus tells you that you can always find him waiting at your Heart Home. You can come whenever you want. You have your Red String, which will always bring you safely to your Heart Home.

You say thank you, and that maybe you'd better start home. Jesus walks with you to where you find the curly end of your Red String.

You and Jesus say goodbye. Do you tell him you'll be back soon?

Then you nudge the curly end of the Red String with the toe of your left foot.

The Red String begins to rewind.

Follow it through the woods to the river. There the Red String works its miracle again, and you get across safely.

Go back through the rocks, around the bushes, under the trees, back toward the field where you started.

Are the animals and birds still there? If they are, maybe you want to wave to them.

Finally, you come back to where the forest and field meet. The Old Woman is still sitting on the big rock.

You thank her for the ball of Red String and hold it up to her.

LET'S GO TO

The Old Woman keeps her hands folded in her lap as she says, "That ball of Red String is yours to keep. Put it in your pocket. That way you can have it whenever you want. All you have to do is reach into your pocket, take out your ball of Red String, hold it in front of your heart and say,

MY HEART HOME!

RED STRING, RED STRING,

I WILL FOLLOW YOU, MY RED STRING.

RED STRING, RED STRING,

LET'S GO TO MY HEART HOME!

Then toss it out in front of you and follow it. You never know what adventures you might have along the way!" You thank her and put the Red String away for now. You are happy knowing it is always there and you can use it whenever you want.

USING THIS MEDITATION WITH CHILDREN

If we think of **prayer** as our **relationship with God,** there are about as many ways to pray as there are to relate to another person. Just as we tell our closest friends things that are going on with us, so we tell God. Just as we listen to our closest friends, so we listen to God. It's one of the best habits to have.

Before starting *The Ball of Red String* with a group of children, you might want to buffer outside noises by playing quiet instrumental music. Then take time to talk about something that has happened recently. If you are in a classroom or religious education situation, it can be a story just read, a lesson just taught, or anything that would be good for the children to think about and incorporate into their prayer lives. Perhaps the children are concerned about an illness or death in the family, an accident, a sick puppy, or a news item. Maybe they are faced with an upcoming event in their lives. Anything of interest to them is good to bring to prayer.

Then follow these steps:

- Review briefly what the children will be bringing to prayer: a story, an event, or a concern.

- Invite the children to get as comfortable as they can. When praying with the children, it is a good idea to do something physically different. If each one has a carpet remnant or if there is a carpeted floor, the children can lie down. Pillows are great for this purpose. Otherwise, position the chairs differently or ask the children how they can do something different for their time with God.

- Suggest that they close their eyes.

- Begin the meditation.

THIS IS WHAT YOU DO

As you guide the mediation, talk with the children as if everything in the narrative is happening right now, for indeed it is—in the imagination of each one, yourself included. Look at the opening words and, as you guide the children to see it, do it yourself! When you are leading the meditation for the first time, it's a good idea to follow the text. As you become more familiar with it, you may want to add your own touches. Take your time; be relaxed.

When the Old Woman throws the ball of Red String, you might pantomime the throw. Or the catch. (Even if the children are lying on the floor with their eyes closed, some will do this themselves. Enjoy them!) Follow the Old Woman's instructions: hold the ball of Red String in front of your heart as you say the words.

As the ball of Red String unwinds through the forest, you may embellish to suit your geography—describe local trees, flowers, animals, and birds. The children will love it! Pause occasionally to give the children time to "see" and "hear" whatever you describe.

The river is a favorite spot. The children must cross the river, and it is wide. However, the Red String is resourceful. Be confident as you tell them, "In some miraculous way, the Red String leads you across the river safely. You even stay dry!" Pause longer here. (After the meditation, if it suits your circumstances, let children draw pictures of how they got across the river and tell one another about them.)

Finally, after the ball of Red String is unwound and only the curly end remains, ask the children to look across the clearing and see their very own Heart Home . . . and Jesus waiting for them. Let your voice reflect the joy and wonder of this. Have Jesus greet them by name.

How Jesus hosts them is also up to you. In the winter, he might have hot chocolate with marshmallows in front of a fireplace; in summer, lemonade on the porch. At this point, you can remind children of what they have talked about or heard before beginning this special time ("Tell Jesus you just heard the story of . . . Tell Jesus that we were talking about . . .").

Or you might want to remind them of the beauty of prayer by saying something like, "You can use words, if you want. But with Jesus, you can just **know** things together. You can invite Jesus to look into your heart and see how you feel." (Children often love it that they don't have to explain.) **Give them time for Jesus to respond to them.** Adapt the words as needed for your situation.

When the conversation is over, Jesus walks them back to the curly end of the Red String. Here they say good-bye, maybe with a hug. Jesus watches them go. Perhaps they look back and wave at each other. It is important that you bring the children back to the place where they started. You might do it more quickly than the journey to the Heart Home, but do go back to the point of origin. Instruct the children to put the ball of Red String in their pocket to be used anytime they wish. Jesus will always be there, waiting for them.

Unless the child wants to talk about it, let the child keep the conversation with Jesus private. In a classroom or group situation, talking about how they got across the river is fine. **It is not advisable, however, to talk about their conversation with Jesus.** You can tell the children that this time with Jesus is private. **Conversations with Jesus are sacred.** Advise them that if there is something they want to talk about, they should tell **one adult** whom they trust. Children will understand privacy and the sacredness of being with Jesus if your tone of voice indicates that this is normal and right. (The need to respect that sacredness and the confidentiality of this time is essential.)

HELPFUL SHORTCUTS

If it is one of those days when everything seems to take longer than planned, here are some shortcuts:

> You do not have to refer to the Old Woman each time, unless you want to remind the children that this is how they got the Red String.

> When the children have held up the ball of Red String, said the words, and tossed it out, it might just lie there for a moment before it weaves itself into a **flying carpet!** Have them hold on tight, enjoy the aerial view, and arrive at their Heart Home more quickly. (Of course, Jesus admires their beautiful carpet. Later you might have them draw it.) After their visit, always bring them back to the starting place and let the Red String form into a ball again.

Or, if using this meditation after a Gospel story, try some applications:

> The Red String might lie on the ground and then—with incredibly fast motions—make itself into a **one-person spaceship.** Inside are Start, Go, Land, and Stop buttons. Always assure children they are safe. Give them directions so they keep together. This allows them to be, for example, at Bethlehem or on the road to Calvary or at the foot of the cross. In essence, this method enables the children to **be present** in whichever Gospel story you were telling before the meditation. They can then talk to Jesus about what the story means to them. (At the end of their conversation, be sure to bring them home and let the Red String rewind and be put away in their pockets.)

> You may make up other approaches or ask the children what **they** wish their Red String would do.

The weather in the meditation can change as well:

> If you want, change the weather to suit the season of the year. If it's very cold or stormy, make sure the children are magically wearing what they need to be comfortable.

ANOTHER VARIATION

Children, as young as five, understand this:

>Sometimes something happens, you don't know what to do, but you find out.

>Sometimes something happens, you know what to do, and you do it.

>Sometimes something happens, you know what to do but don't want to.

>**Sometimes something happens, you know what to do, you are willing, but you are just not up to it.**

This time of not being up to it is something to bring to Jesus in a very special way. After asking the children to think of a time like this, take them to their Heart Home. After they have greeted Jesus, encourage the children to tell him what they are not able to do. Maybe they are walking with Jesus. Maybe they are sitting together by the lake or on a rock.

After they tell Jesus what it is, suggest they lean against him, as John did at the Last Supper. Let Jesus' courage and strength, love and compassion, wisdom and peace flow into them. Give a longer pause here; there is no need for words.

When they are ready, they walk back to the end of the Red String. Remind them (or let Jesus remind them) that they may have to come more than once to **be up to it,** but that Jesus is always there waiting and ready to give them his full attention. He loves it when they come to be with him!

AT-HOME ADAPTATIONS

The Ball of Red String is also an excellent tool for family prayer at bedtime or together in the evening. It's delightful when the whole family prays together about the same thing: a celebration, a problem, a decision to be made, a family concern. Whatever it is, it can be identified before starting the meditation, just as one would do in using *The Ball of Red String* with a group of children.

Or there may be a special time when you say the following prayer before the meditation:

> Jesus, we are always coming to you to tell you about us. Suppose this time we ask you to tell us about you.

Then, in Jesus' presence, each listens with his or her own heart. Jesus sometimes speaks in the language of silence. Before beginning, you might encourage the child or the family members to expect to wait. Waiting is not a favorite pastime in our culture. We need to wait on God just as we wait for flowers to bloom, crops to ripen, and spring to come. Some things take time. Silent prayer is one of them.